Rivers and Streams

Anita Ganeri

www.raintreepublishers.co.uk
Visit our website to find out more information about Raintree books.

To order:
Phone 0845 6044371
Fax +44 (0) 1865 312263
Email myorders@raintreepublishers.co.uk

Customers from outside the UK please telephone +44 1865 312262

Raintree is an imprint of Capstone Global Library Limited, a company incorporated in England and Wales having its registered office at 7 Pilgrim Street, London, EC4V 6LB – Registered company number: 6695582

First published in hardback in 2010
Ppaperback edition first published in 2011

Edited by Charlotte Guillain, Nancy Dickmann, and Catherine Veitch
Designed by Joanna Hinton-Malivoire
Picture research by Elizabeth Alexander and Ruth Blair
Original illustrations © Capstone Global Library
Original illustrations by Joanna Hinton-Malivoire (pp. 28, 29)
Production by Victoria Fitzgerald
Originated by Capstone Global Library Ltd
Printed and bound in China by Leo Paper Products

ISBN 978 0 431 17242 2 (hardback)
14 13 12 11 10
10 9 8 7 6 5 4 3 2 1

ISBN 978 0 431 17249 1 (paperback)
15 14 13 12 11
10 9 8 7 6 5 4 3 2 1

British Library Cataloguing in Publication Data
Ganeri, Anita
Rivers and streams. -- (Nature trails)
577.6'4-dc22

Acknowledgements
We would like to thank the following for permission to reproduce photographs: Alamy pp. **4-5** (© Terry Mathews), **6** (© Paul Glendell), **10** (© ICP), **12** (© imagebroker), **17** (© Wolfgang Pölzer), **18** (© 22DigiTal), **27** (© Paul Glendell); Corbis pp. **9** (© Bernd Vogel), **14** (© Steve Austin; Papilio), **22** (© Dennis Johnson; Papilio), **26** (© Lars Langemeier/A.B.); iStockphoto pp. **11** (© Neill Staniforth), **25** (© Andrew Howe), **24** (© Andy Gehrig); Naturepl p. **16** (© Willem Kolvoort); Shutterstock pp. **15** (© alle), **20** (© Karel Gallas), **23** (© Borislav Borisov), **13 left** (© Marcos Carvalho), **13 right** (© Ivonne Wierink).

Cover photograph of Glen Shiel, north west Highlands, Scotland, reproduced with permission of Corbis (© John Miller/ Robert Harding World Imagery).

The publisher would like to thank Emma Shambrook for her assistance in the preparation of this book.

Contents

Any words appearing in the text in bold, **like this**, are explained in the glossary.

What are rivers and streams?

A river is a large stretch of **fresh water** that moves or flows along. A stream is like a river but it is much smaller. Some rivers flow quite slowly. Others are fast-flowing.

Rivers and streams are types of **habitats**. A habitat is a place where plants and animals live. Many different plants and animals live in and around rivers in Britain.

In this book, the Signpost boxes ask you to find out more about animals and plants. Ask an adult to help you find information in books at school, in the library, or on the Internet.

Parts of a river

Most rivers start as small **springs** or streams high up on hillsides. Several streams join together to form a fast-flowing river. The water carries rocks and mud along with it.

This river makes loops called **meanders** as it flows along.

The journey of a river

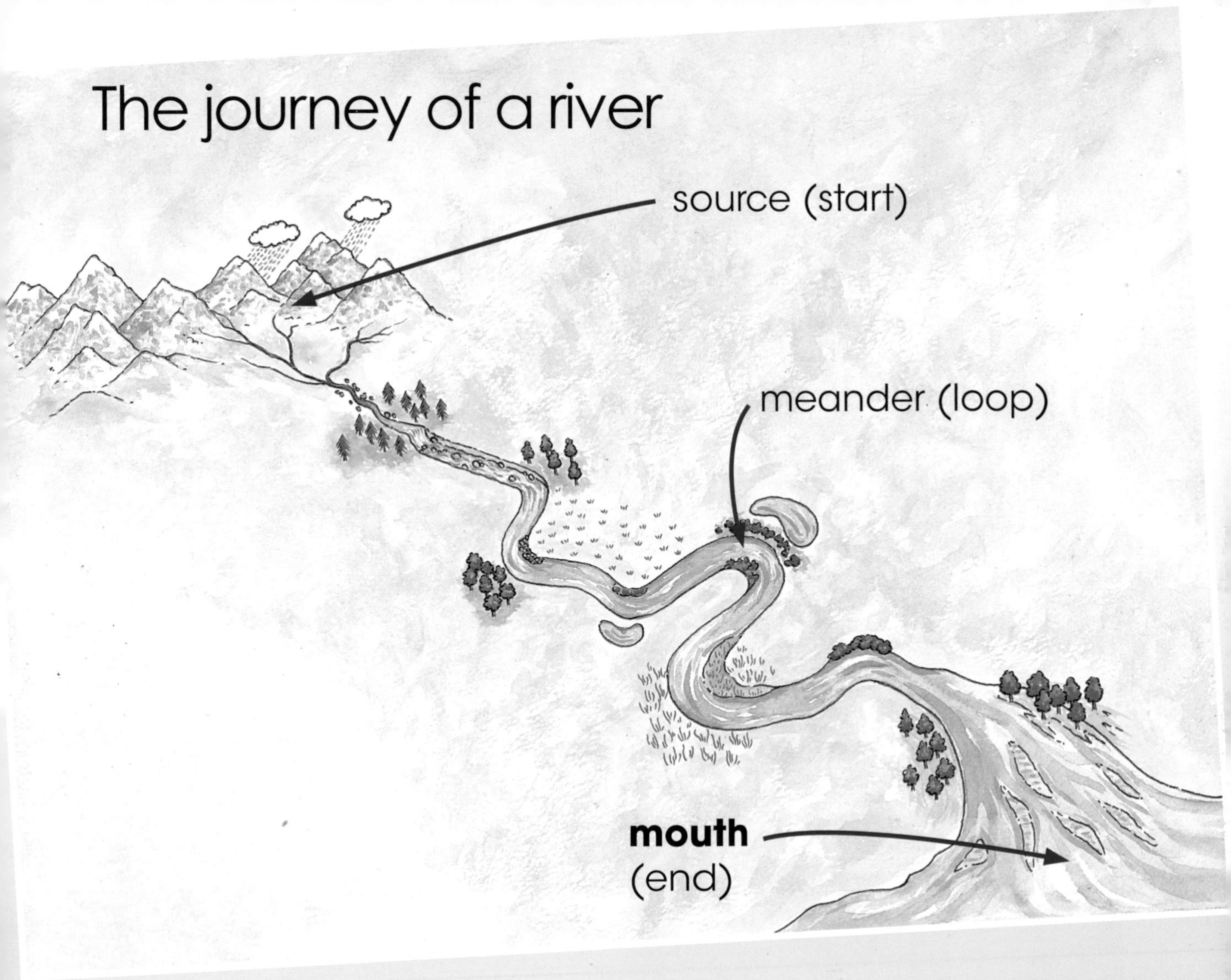

As the river reaches flatter ground, it slows down. Some of the rocks and mud sinks to the bottom. The river becomes wider and deeper. Finally, it flows into the sea.

Exploring rivers and streams

Rivers and streams are great places to explore. Look for plants and animals living in the water and along the bank. Their watery habitat is always moving, and they can easily get swept away. Many have special **features** to help them **survive**.

What to take with you

- ✓ A fishing net
- ✓ A bucket or jar, filled with river water
- ✓ A smaller, white plastic pot, filled with river water, for looking at interesting finds
- ✓ A spoon for moving animals into the pot and back into the river
- ✓ A magnifying glass
- ✓ A notebook and pencil

The best time to explore rivers is in the spring and summer.

STAY SAFE

- Always take an adult with you when you visit a river or stream.
- Do not get too close to the edge of the river, or you could fall in.
- Wash your hands after water activities and cover up any cuts.

Riverside plants

Many different kinds of plants live along rivers. Riverbanks have soft, damp soil. As the river flows, it can wash some of the bank away. Riverbank plants need strong roots to hold them firmly in place.

Slow-flowing rivers leave mud and soil along their banks. Plants, such as reeds and irises, take **root** in this mud. You can see them growing in large clumps.

More river plants

Some plants live in the river itself. They have special features, such as different types of leaves, to help them survive in the flowing water. In a fast-flowing river, bur-reed grows long, floating leaves that trail on the surface.

Count and record

Can you count some of the different types of river plants? Spend ten minutes counting, then record what you see in a tally chart like this one.

Plant	Number spotted
Weeping willow	II
Purple loosestrife	III
Water lily	~~IIII~~ ~~IIII~~ I
Common reed	~~IIII~~ ~~IIII~~ ~~IIII~~ III
Yellow iris	~~IIII~~
Arrowhead	IIII

weeping willow

purple loosestrife

Ask an adult to help you look up these plants on the Internet.

River insects

Stonefly nymphs squeeze their bodies into tiny cracks in the rocks so they do not get swept away by the flowing water.

There are many different types of river insects. Look in the air, on the water's surface and in the water itself. The best time to spot insects is in the spring or early summer.

It is difficult for insects to live in fast-flowing rivers. The moving water can easily carry them away because they are so small. Some survive by living in the mud on the **riverbed**. Others shelter under rocks or among the plants.

Can you find out some more about river insects?

- dragonfly
- gnat
- caddis fly (adult)

Caddis fly larvae make cases out of tiny stones to keep them safe.

More small creatures

Many other small creatures live in rivers and streams. River snails live underwater and feed on water plants. They breathe by taking in **oxygen** from the water.

Crayfish and shrimps hide among the rocks and stones on the riverbed. At night, crayfish crawl along the bottom, feeding on fish and other small animals.

STAY SAFE

- Never hurt river animals or pull up plants.
- If you catch something in your net, put it straight into your bucket.
- Use the spoon to put anything interesting into your plastic pot. Then put it back into the river as quickly as possible.

Fish in rivers and streams

Different types of fish live in rivers, although they can be difficult to spot. Look out for dark shapes swimming through the water. You might see fish, such as minnows, that swim in groups.

Minnows swim in groups to protect themselves from larger fish and birds.

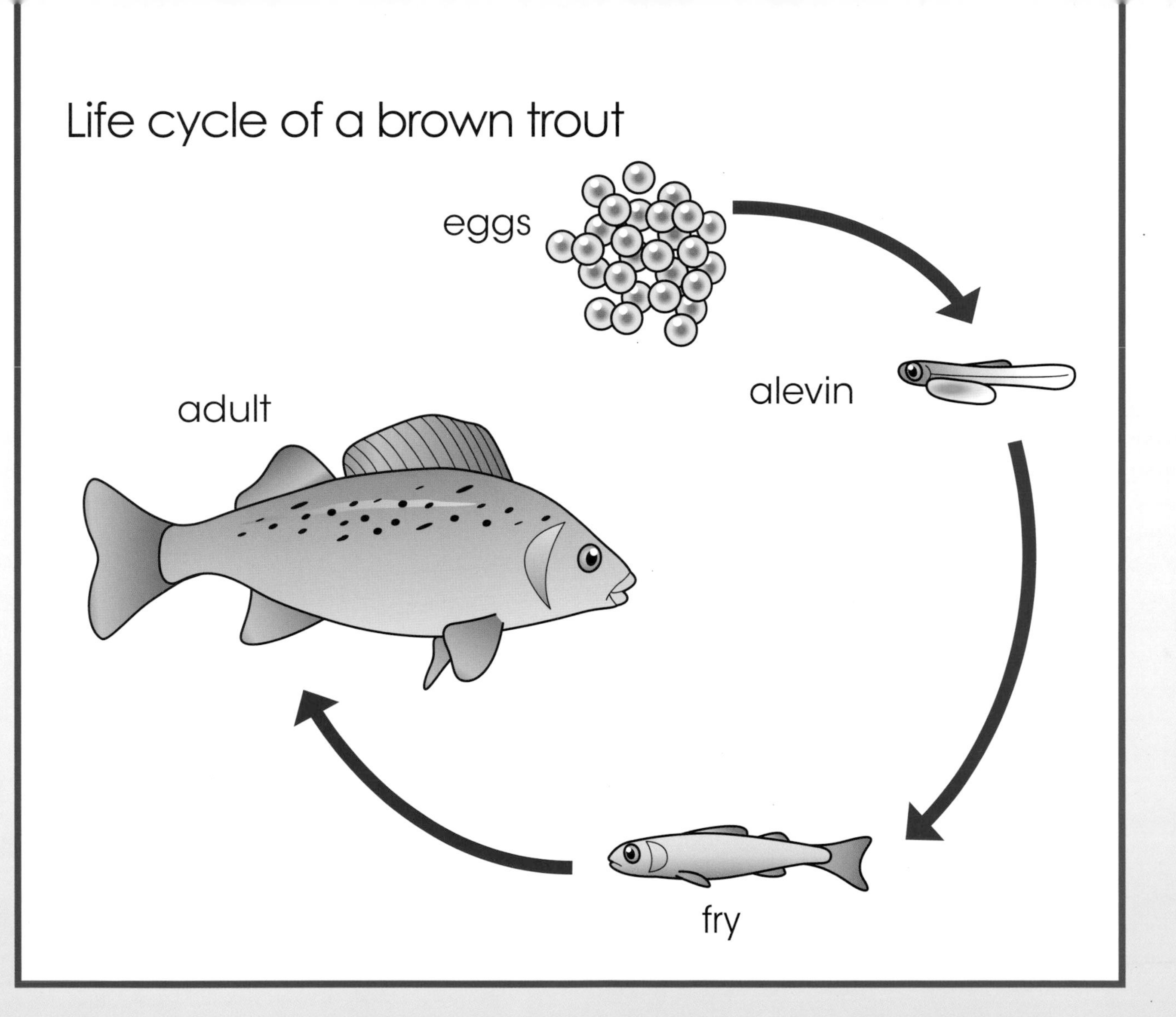

Trout live in fast-flowing streams. They lay their eggs in the gravel on the stream bed. The eggs hatch into **alevins** that grow into young fish, called **fry**. The fry grow into adult trout.

Birds of rivers and streams

Birds come to rivers and streams to drink, wash, and find their food. Many river birds such as kingfishers catch water insects and fish to eat.

The best time to go bird-watching is early in the morning. Pick a spot by the riverbank, then sit quietly and wait. Look for birds on branches above the water and in the plants growing along the riverbank.

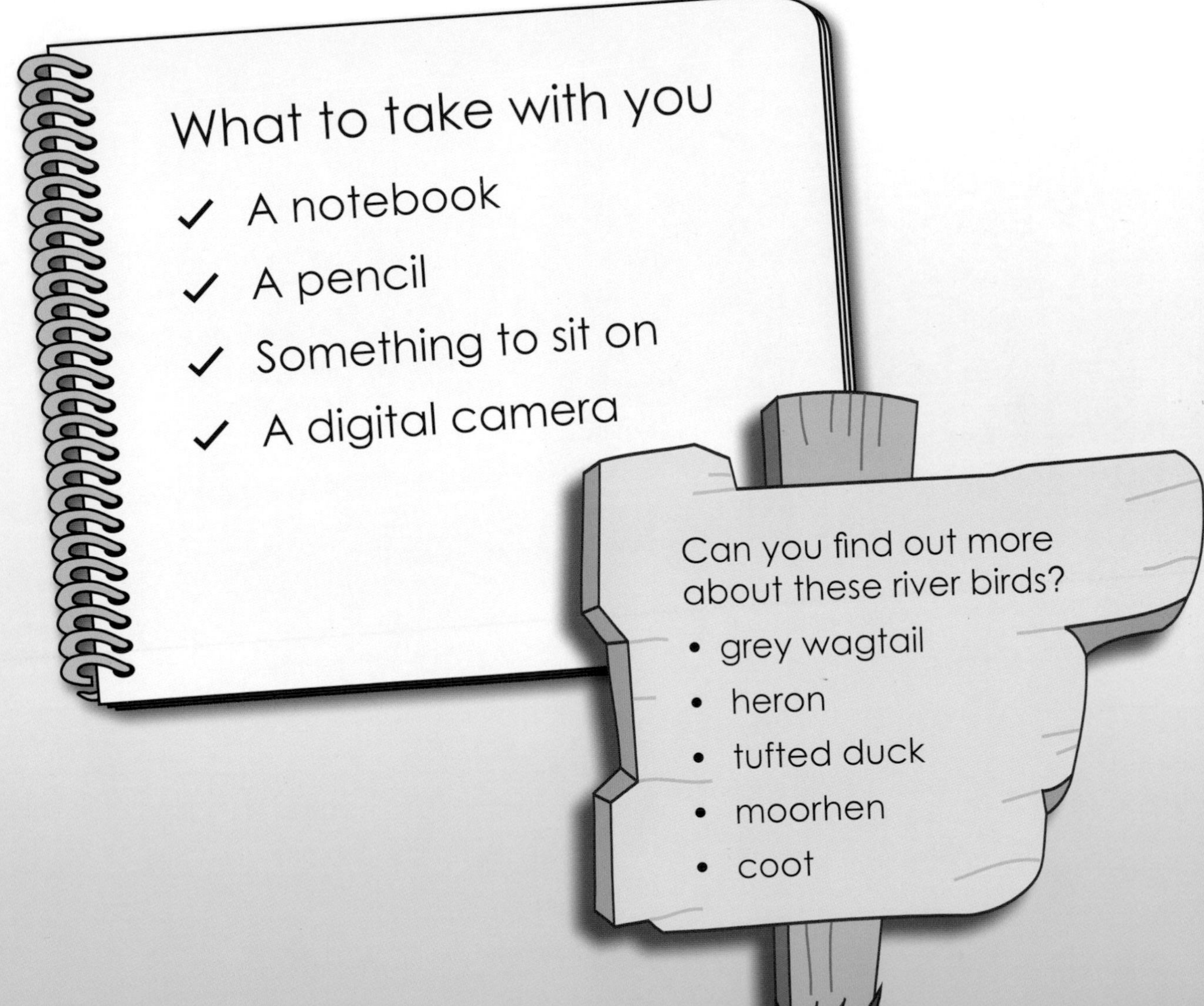

More river birds

The reed warbler builds its nest from grass and reed flowers.

Rivers also give many places where birds can build their nests. The reed warbler builds its nest among the reeds along the riverbank. The nest is very deep so that the eggs and chicks do not fall out when the wind blows the reeds.

The dipper builds its nest among rocks, under bridges, or behind waterfalls close to a river or stream. The dome-shaped nest is made from moss and grass.

River mammals

Mammals, such as otters, also come to rivers to drink and eat. Otters catch fish in the water to eat. They have long, streamlined bodies, **webbed** toes, and waterproof fur to help them swim.

Baby water voles learn to swim when they are about a month old.

Look out for a hole in the riverbank. It could be the entrance to a water vole's burrow. Inside, the water vole builds a nest lined with grass.

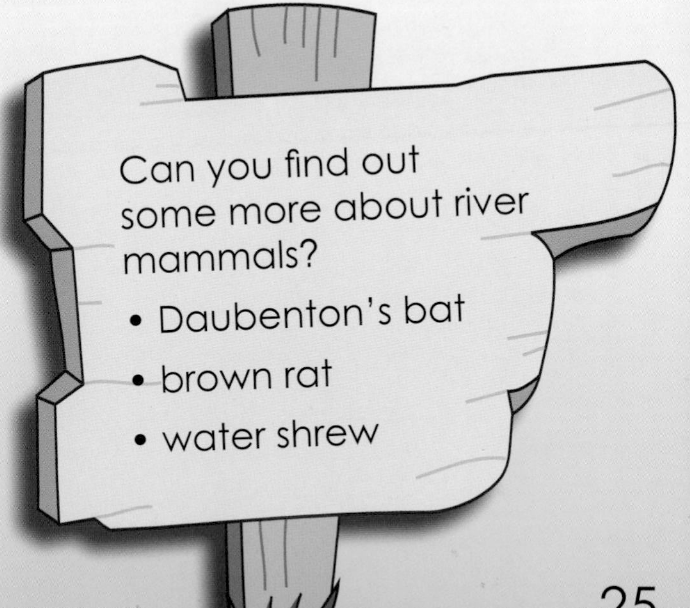

Rivers and streams in danger

Many rivers and streams are in danger. Factories and farms pour **chemicals** into the water. The chemicals kill river plants and animals. People throw rubbish into the water. Oil can leak from boats using the river.

This river has been **polluted** with chemicals.

You can help look after rivers and streams by taking care when you visit them. Never leave any rubbish behind and clear up any litter you find lying around. Wear thick gloves to do this, and ask an adult to help.

More things to do

There are a lot more things you can do by a river or stream.

River walk logbook

Next time you go for a walk by a river, take your notebook with you. Sketch any animals you see and write a short description. Note down the animal's colour, size, shape, and special features, and where you found it. Use a field guide or information from the Internet to identify the animals when you get home.

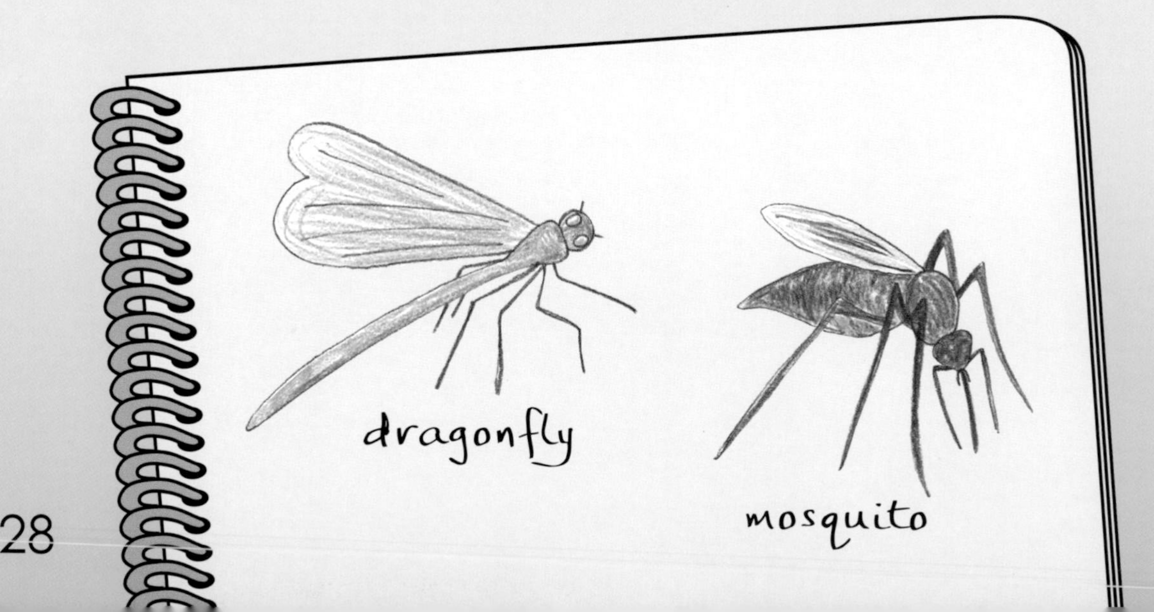

River insects match up

Many young water insects look very different to the adult insects. Young water insects are called **nymphs** or **larvae**.

Can you match up each nymph below with the correct adult?

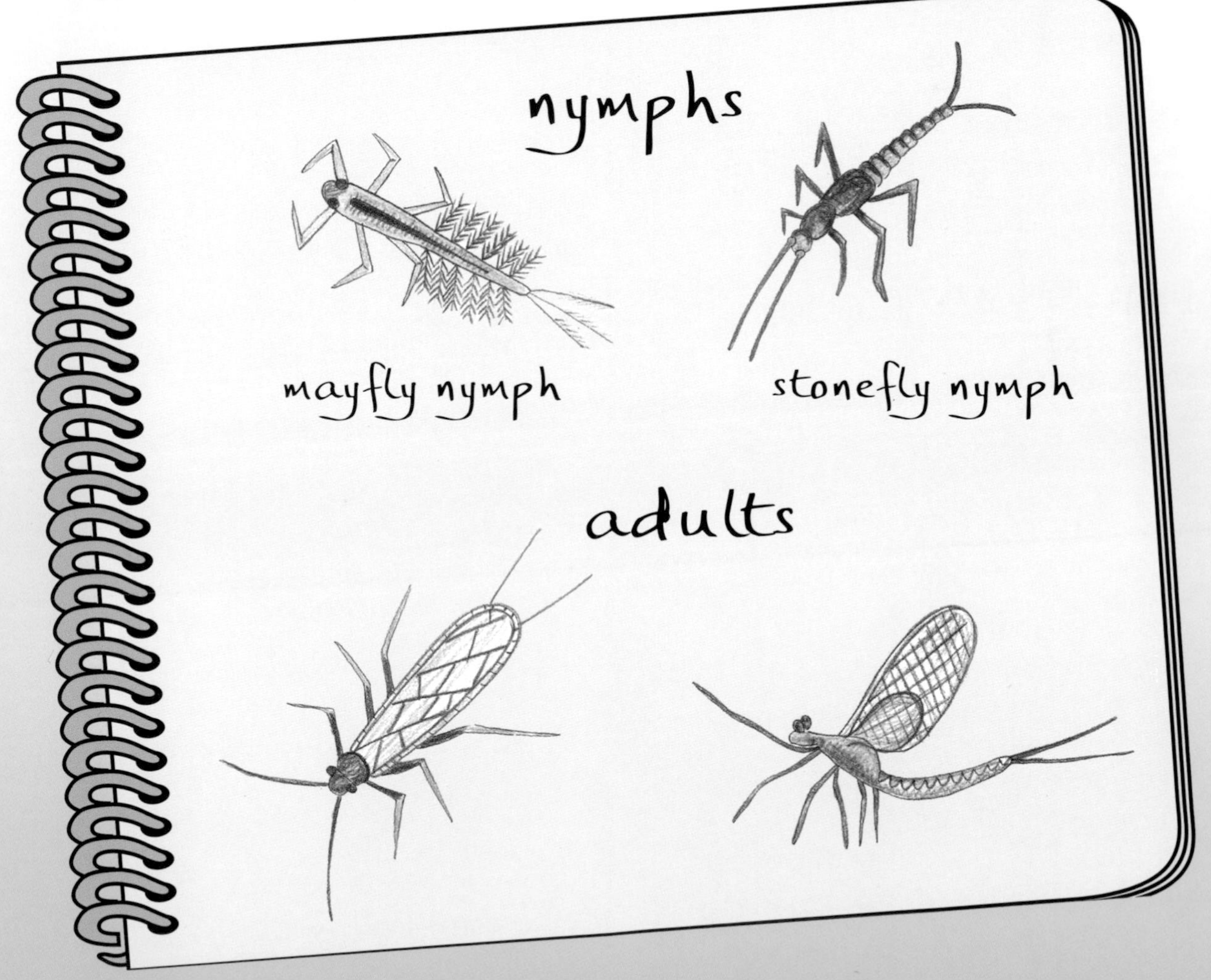

Answer: the mayfly is on the right, the stonefly is on the left.

Glossary

alevins tiny fish-like creatures that hatch out of eggs

chemicals substances that are used in making and growing things

features special parts of a plant's or animal's body that helps it survive

fresh water water in ponds, lakes and rivers, that is not salty

fry young fish

habitats places where plants and animals live

larvae young of some insects, such as caddis flies

mammals animals that have hair and feed their babies on milk

meander large bend or curve in a river

mouth place where a river flows into the sea

nymphs young of some insects, such as dragonflies

oxygen gas that living things need to live

polluted made dirty by rubbish or chemicals

riverbed bottom of a river

roots parts of a plant that grow down into the ground

source place where a river begins

spring where water gushes up from underground

survive be able to live

webbed feet that have skin stretched between the toes or claws

Find out more

Books to read

Investigating Rivers, Clare Hibbert (Evans Brothers, 2005)

Eyewitness: Pond and River, Steve Parker (Dorling Kindersley, 2003)

Websites and organizations

UK Rivers Network
www.ukrivers.net
This organization encourages people to look after rivers through clean-up projects and campaigns.

Young People's Trust for the Environment
www.ypte.org.uk
This charity aims to encourage young people's understanding of the environment.

The Wildlife Trusts
www.wildlifetrusts.org
This voluntary organization is dedicated to looking after Britain's wildlife and habitats.

Index